THE WHISPERS SERIES

ABOUT MY GIRLFRIEND

Compiled and edited by Kate Johnson

Illustrations by Jim Lefevre

Nightingale
An imprint of Wimbledon Publishing Company
LONDON

Copyright © 2000
Illustrations © 2000

First published in Great Britain in 2000
by Wimbledon Publishing Company Ltd
P.O. Box 9779 London SW19 7ZG
All rights reserved

First published 2000 in Great Britain

ISBN: 1903222 21 4

Produced in Great Britain
Printed and bound in Hungary

From passion and lust, to fights and compromise, the book looks at love from the man's perspective and reveals the important feelings that he often leaves bubbling under the surface.

This book is the voice of these deep emotions. It's a book of secrets.

Kate Johnson
1999

The Moment

'She stood up in a crowded room. I was attracted to her, but not in love. I fell in love six months later when we kissed and both fell over in the street. Seriously!'

Eric, 29

'It started with friendship and lust. I wouldn't have it any other way. No-one's really fallen in love with me at first sight; I tend to grow on people. I can fall in love at first sight, but that's only falling in love with the idea of someone - who you think they are - and not who they really are.'

Joel, 28

'I got so used to pursuing her, and being knocked back, I never thought anything would happen. One night we went out for a drink and I decided I'd give up on her; it had gone on too long, and it was hopeless. I think she sensed that and she kissed me, and that's how it all started.'

Ray, 28

'You know you're in love when you get jealous and psychotic about anyone who comes into contact with her, including the man who delivers her post.'

Andy, 35

'I didn't fall in love suddenly, it was a build up of emotions. I felt like a branch floating down stream, and the river was being stopped by sandbanks. When I said that I loved her, it felt like the sandbanks burst and all my feelings gushed out.'

Ashley, 25

'You can think of a partner on paper, and make a mental list, which is how I do lots of things. Compatibility can't be put on paper. You never know who you'll fit with. It's chemistry and timing - meeting the right person and being ready. And no, my girlfriend doesn't fit my mental list!'

Jonathan, 34

'It started with lust. It should be immediate chemistry or nothing. Friendship ruins the sense of otherness.'
Alan, 36

'I look for compassion and passion. Not necessarily in that order.'
Marcus, 30

'I was shot down for 9 months, but I enjoyed the thrill of the chase, and any man who says he doesn't is lying!'

Joel, 28

'It happened so quickl - it was something magnetic, and intuitive, an elusive feeling. I couldn't pin down the feeling, and I couldn't explain it. I still can't!'

Ed, 30

'It got more serious when I moved away, she was a lot more interested when I wasn't around all the time. I realised I'd been making it too easy for her!'

Sam, 28

'I knew I was in love the first time we kissed - I was shaking.'

Michael, 28

'I knew I was in love because when we argued, instead of forgetting about her, I'd be depressed for days until we kissed and made up and then I was happy again.'

Phil, 35

ROMANCE

'Romance is important, because it keeps things going. I send flowers, cook surprise dinners, organise weekends away. We behave like we're dating even though it's been a long time.'

David, 35

'I only ever do romantic things; they aren't done for me. I once cooked a surprise meal at home for Valentine's day, and she had dirty feet. She's the girl with dirty feet - that makes it sound romantic doesn't it?'

James, 27

'I'm told it's romantic to cook. I reached the height of my culinary wits when I cooked a shepherd's pie and inscribed our initials on the top, in potato.'

Philip, 35

'It's romantic when she tells me a secret, and lying in bed whispering to each other is romantic. But then it's hard, when you argue, not to use the same secrets against them.'

John, 28

'Flowers and dinners are romantic, I guess. Romance to me is being told that she loves me, that she trusts me and that I trust her. Emotional commitment is romantic.'

Lee, 25

'I'm a hopeless romantic. I do romantic things as a surprise. I give flowers for no reason, but never after a row to make up.'

Christopher, 24

'I like doing romantic things, like surprise holidays, but it seems to be misinterpreted as me trying to be in control all the time.'

Paul, 38

'Romance is embarrassing. It's too overt. As I've got older I've become more caring, which is more discreet, but it doesn't translate well into romantic gestures.'

Andrew, 40

'I'm totally romantic, materially and spiritually. She took me babysitting. We were watching a video with the two-year-old on the bed. He didn't understand a word, and he fell asleep on one arm. Then she fell asleep on the other arm and I was pinned to the bed, trapped...

'...It was wonderful, it was the moment I knew I was in love; I thought this could be the future.'

Tom, 30

'I get nothing romantic from her, but she's exceedingly attentive and cuddly and touch-feely and sensitive. I organise romantic getaways, it's a great way to spend time together. I guess I benefit because I'm involved too, so it's not selfless romance. Would I send her to a spa - maybe, but what's in it for me?'

Keith, 31

'Romance to me isn't dinner, flowers, chocolates or presents, it's emotional intimacy and commitment. She trusts me, and I trust her; that's romantic.'

Lee, 25

'Romance is important - if she was as pragmatic and practical as me, it wouldn't work. She's a hopeless romantic, and I pretend I don't like it, but I know deep down that I do.'

Joel, 28

'I'm romantic; when a love song comes on the radio, I'll say, "This is my song to you". She'll say "Mmm...you still haven't taken the rubbish out have you?" She does it on purpose, and it always makes me laugh.'

Ray, 37

FRIENDSHIP

'Most men have no concept of friendship with women. If we are friends with women, we're just biding our time.'

Christian, 45

'Friendship is age-related. I think friendship between men and women is probably more important as you get older.'

Edward, 28

'She's not my best friend. Friendship is key, but it's also good to be able to discover new things about each other. Time apart is just as important as good times together.'

Anthony, 23

'She's definitely my best friend. If she wasn't, we wouldn't survive time apart.'

Dominic, 25

'Her friendship is the most important thing that I get from her. Possibly it's because men don't have really close friends. If I confided my worst fears to my male friends, they'd say, "That's awful - another beer?"'

Charles, 26

'Friendship is definitely the main component of our relationship. She didn't start out as my best friend, but she became it, partly because of longevity, and partly because she's patient and more inclined to put up with my bad moods (I'm a moody bastard). Lots of friends wouldn't.'

Joel, 28

Friction

'It's not as hard to compromise as it was at the beginning. I let a lot of little things that used to grate go. I've learned to pick my battles.'

Russell, 28

'The hardest part of having a relationship is overcoming your insecurity about whether the relationship will last. You have to force yourself to be brave. When I said, "I love you" I was so nervous before saying it I nearly passed out!'

Bob, 25

'Relationships develop or die. It's very difficult to give up your independence. I had to make a decision. Did I want to be in this or not? Obviously I did. So moving forward wasn't that big an eye opener, because I had given it a lot of thought.'

Steve, 28

'I find it really annoying when we plan to visit a friend of hers, and she still spends the day before talking to her on the phone for hours. In my mind, that would leave you with nothing to say the next day.'

Phillip, 35

'I wanted to watch a big football match, and put the TV on with the volume down. She made it clear that conversation was the preferred option. Now I don't sneak the TV on, I say, "This is on at 8.00 (and we're watching it)."'

Adrian, 30

'You don't have to do everything together. I love going to football matches with my mates, without her. She was envious that I had a hobby I loved so passionately - and that she didn't have anything like that. I said, "But you do, you have shopping."'

Neil, 23

'I haven't given up my independence, but I've had to adapt. I've given myself to one person, but I don't feel I've sacrificed anything. Sharing life's experiences with someone you love is enjoyable. We're going travelling together soon - being independent together!'

David, 22

'I'm not good at forgiving and forgetting, but I do try and understand her, and I'm getting better at tolerating all her other commitments. I see myself as an individual, not half of someone else; we are an important part - but not the only part - of each other's lives.'

Lee, 25

'We had a big argument - I smashed a bottle of wine and she told me to grow up. We both stormed off in different directions. The next day I sent her a tin of macaroni and cheese to say sorry. I knew she hated macaroni and cheese, so I thought it would be something she could keep forever.'

Simon, 38

'We don't row, but we faff around and disagree.'

Paul, 27

'I'm not observant enough to notice her faults, although I do notice her nagging and her suspicious mind - which is her intuition. I find that especially annoying, usually because when she's suspicious, she's absolutely right to be.'

Richard, 38

'I don't notice details. She finds that irritating - but it has a positive side. I overlook her putting on weight, or lying around with dirty hair in her tracksuit.'

George, 29

'She's much better than me at arguing: she holds back in battle. That's not my forte; I say what comes to mind and ask for forgiveness later.'

Daniel, 32

'It's hard to deal with the baggage that other people come with. Their families, their relationship history, their expectations and experience. But that's what makes them what they are.'

William, 38

'It's important to remember when you're fighting that maybe it's no-one's fault. Maybe you've had a bad week at work - it's important to find out the root cause. Then it's easier to move on and make new mistakes!'

David, 35

'The hardest part is having to think for two, and to include someone else in all your plans. My secret for success? I don't have one.'

Joel, 28

'The hardest part is maintaining interest. The best part is coming home.'

Ernest, 61

'The hardest part is getting over the ideas that I had about love. I thought falling in love would be simple but it's not. You don't fall in love and live happily ever after. I hate that!'

Roger, 45

'The hardest part is to trust someone; it takes a long time to develop and it's broken very easily.'

Tony, 29

'Do I forgive and forget? There's nothing to forgive.'

Ernest, 61

'It's really important to be calm when you argue. Only when you talk about things rationally, and try to solve the problem, do you realise how neurotic you have been.'

Lee, 25

'I was always very mean when we argued. I'm learning not to be, but in the meantime I'm getting very good at apologising - I get so much practise.'

Sean, 29

'You can learn to compromise by learning what's important to the other person. If you are nonchalant, it's easier to get your way. You say, "I don't mind". She says, "Neither do I". You say, "How about this?" She says, 'OK.' But if you said, "We'll do this", she'd say, "No way."'

Tom, 30

'I've lost a lot of my independence, but it doesn't seem to matter any more. I've learnt to use plural words. And I get really irritated when she still says, 'I' and not 'we' all the time.'

Thomas, 28

'The worst thing about having a relationship is the fighting, but then the best thing is making up. If you have a passionate relationship, you have to take the highs and lows.'

Jason, 26

'She makes everything more fun. Losing my way when I'm driving is a huge trauma for me, but with her I burst out laughing.'

Thomas, 34

'What do I know about love - virtually nothing. I'm constantly learning about it.'

Rick, 22

'We can talk about anything, for hours. And even when one of us hangs up, the other calls back immediately, usually to say something trivial.'

Jack, 18

'I love her because she still makes home-made elderflower cordial.'

Philip, 35

'The best part is that I can be myself, and call about anything. It removes all burden of making decisions because I can decide everything by a council of two.'

Tom, 30

'I knew she loved me when she lent me her car. Forget cooking meals, it's the wheels that count!'

Gregory, 37

'I knew I was in love when I sensed all of a sudden that I was terrified of losing her. It had never occurred to me before.'

David, 35

'I love her because when I'm with her, I want to be a better person.'

Alastair, 25

'She's only inept when she wants to be. She can turn from innocent and hopeless to someone who could command armies in two minutes.'

Richard, 28

Lessons Learnt

'Love is friendship caught fire.'
> Dean, 26

'Lust brought us together and love keeps us together.'
> Lawrence, 31

'You can have good sex anytime, but making love is great sex.'
> Matthew, 35

'The way to a girl's heart is to love her pets. You know you're in if her dog likes you. So force yourself to act as though her horrible, dirty pet that seems to snarl at you all the time is the sweetest thing on God's earth.'
> Sam, 28

'You learn to ride out the bad bits, and the good bits should come naturally.'

Colin, 27

'Love is like a bank, you have to build up savings, so that when things go wrong, you fall back on some of your savings. You might even get overdrawn. But afterwards you have to work really hard at putting more money in the bank.'

Harry, 30

'You look for years for the one person who will really love you, and when you find them, you can't believe that they, of all people, would chose to love you. When someone says they love you, you should accept it, and be grateful for it, and not try to prove them wrong.'

Michael, 28

'If you think you're in love with someone you should make a list of all their faults. Qualities tend to fade, whilst the faults will get more pronounced as a relationship wears on. If you learn to deal with the faults, you can stay together.'

Tony, 58

'True love is very rare. It's rare to meet someone you're passionate, intimate and comfortable with. - especially when those sentiments are reciprocated!'

Chris, 27

'You can't hold on to something by force. It's either yours by right, by universal law, or it's not. You can hold on to someone by demonstrating and showing your love, being considerate and showing warmth and empathy, and proving that you care what they're about.'

Simon, 22

'I still don't understand why it is that everywhere I go in the world with my girlfriend, she says, "I must just pop into Boots."'

Rory, 37

'I believe in love at first sight, and you can grow into being friends if you find there is anything left beyond infatuation.'

Patrick, 26

'If you're really in love, you can't fall out of love, or you never loved them in the first place.'

William, 21

'There's never a good time to say, "I love you." You can't say it after she tells you, because it sounds like you're just being polite. But then you know from that moment on she's waiting to hear it.'

Tony, 25

'Being with someone usually means that you have to share everything, like bank accounts, for example!'

Dominic, 25

'Ignore all the rules. Avoiding relationships because you - or the other person - are on the rebound is rubbish.'

Dominic, 25

'She shouldn't get worried about small infidelities. It would be something to worry about if I fell in love with someone else, because you can't control that, and you can't compete with that. But I haven't so far.'

James, 39

'Women are more independent than men, but there are still power struggles in a relationship. Now it's not about who pays for the pizza, it's about who calls to place the order, and decides what toppings.'

Simon, 38

'I've learned that persistence pays. And love is remarkably forgiving; you can do stupid things, and behave badly, and if you love someone and they love you, you get a second chance.'

Joel, 28